FOR

_____

This book is for you.

WITH LOVE

_____

The

UNIVERSE
LISTENS *to*
Brave

HOW COURAGE
WILL CHANGE
YOUR LIFE

REBECCA RAY

For Ronny,
who believed in my wings
before I knew I had them.

For Nyssa,
who introduced me to real love
and infinite courage.

For Bennett,
the breath, heart and voice of a million universes,
and the creation of our brave love.

CONTENTS

DEAR READER

Please know that this book has been written for you: the ones who feel. The ones who care. The ones who lead with their heart. We are on the path, doing our utmost to stay there, authentically, truthfully, willingly. Getting a little lost at times, but always returning.

This book is for us: the ones who keeping coming back to brave.

I believe you'll arrive at these pages when the time is right for you. When you need a place to find your courage. When you want to hold this courage and feel it in your hands. When you want to continue the conversation about what's important to you outside your head.

Between the covers of this book is your place to rest, rebuild, rise.

Reach for this book when you need an intention for your day. Or when you're weighing up a decision to act and the space in between here and there feels overwhelming. Or, especially when you're in the middle of doing the work of healing, or grieving, or creating, or learning to love yourself and you need to be reminded to keep going, that brave is worth every ounce of effort.

Perhaps these pages are gifted to you from someone who recognises your courage. Or perhaps you're the messenger and this book finds you, so you can deliver it to a friend who needs to know that their courage is seen, too.

The notes of brave you're about to contemplate are not promises for a better life. This is not a book of answers. You won't find the perfect antidote to all your pain here. But you will find pieces of yourself in these pages – and pieces of me, too – and pieces of all the footsteps we take on the path of the brave souls.

This is your invitation to come back to your bravest self. I see you. I'm with you.

Rebecca xo

Introduction

BRAVE (AGAIN)

*W*e were three days into the autumn of 1998. The season had turned quickly, a gentle chill introducing itself to the air at 6 am. You might say that the sky was the blue of Twitter's little bird, but you wouldn't because Twitter didn't yet exist. On this day though, the sky was definitely a Twitterish shade.

I was 18 and self-medicating a too-familiar, gnawing anxiety by taking flying lessons (because the scientifically supported treatment for adolescent angst is to pilot a small piece of tin beyond one's own limitations, isn't it?)

Well, I had to do *something*. Doing nothing was unacceptable because it meant just sitting with the feelings of anxiety. And I did my best to reserve all the seats at my 'Feelings Table' for the emotions that I liked. I tiptoed around the emotions I wasn't so fond of, trying not to make eye contact, the way you do with bullies at school. And just like school bullies, those uncomfortable feelings inevitably muscled their way onto the table and claimed a seat. The feelings we don't like always seem entitled and smug in the way they arrive and demand attention. But at 18, I wasn't ready to lift my head up and face them. I was seeking a way to obliterate them altogether.

I was searching for my peace.

This time, I decided to do something so brave (to my

mind) that my emotional tormentors would be awed into submission by my strength. I would do something so big that they would have no choice but to surrender and leave me alone. If I had to, I could push myself just this once if it meant afterwards I'd get a break from the fear.

My grandfather told me flying was no harder than driving a car. For him, maybe. But to a non-mathematically minded, spatially challenged, doing-it-to-kick-anxiety-to-the-curb kind of person, that wasn't quite true.

It wasn't the mechanical act of flying that was so hard. It was bargaining with the claws around my oesophagus and the dread thumping at the walls of my stomach that was arduous.

Touching down on the third circuit, my flying instructor directed me to taxi to one side of the runway. A steady and conscientious guy named Lou, he was too tall for the cockpit we shared but managed to fold himself into the space in a way that reminded me of the children's character Gumby. I don't think Lou knew about the Feelings Table, or that I was flying to prove something to Anxiety – and its cronies Self-doubt and

'If I had to, I could push myself just this once if it meant afterwards I'd get a break from the fear.'

Not Good Enough, and occasionally Self-loathing, too –
once and for all.

I did as I was told, despite my stomach contents threat-
ening to leave home prematurely. Lou nodded at me and
said, 'You're ready. Be brave, Beck.' And with that, he extri-
cated himself from the Cessna 150 and ambled over to the
control tower, leaving me in command of the aircraft, his
reputation, and my life.

How I wished gravity would save me right then and
there. Fear is like that. It paralyses our potential, our spirit,
our hope. Fear robs us of wings. If we let it.

My knees shook, making taxiing in a straight line to the
holding point almost impossible. Stating my intentions
over the radio to the tower seemed simple enough, until
I opened my mouth to discover my tongue was dusty and
my throat acidic. Despite the screaming in my head – 'I'm
not ready, not with only eight hours of practice, and I'm not
good enough, I'll never be good enough, don't you understand?' – an air traffic controller with a
firm, you-will-do-this voice cleared me
for take-off.

So, I took off. And I completed the
circuit. And I touched down gently on
the runway. And I didn't crash and die,

'How I wished gravity
would save me right
then and there. Fear is
like that. It paralyses
our potential, our spirit,
our hope. Fear robs us
of wings. If we let it.'

or worse, embarrass Lou.

Suck on that, Anxiety.

It was then that my ego smoked me out with a high so convincing that I believed I'd done my One Brave Thing.

From now on, I would belong to the fearless ones.

Ready for anything.

Untouchable by the uncomfortable feelings.

My emotional naivete feels awkward even as I write this. I don't need to tell you what happened next, because I'm sure you can see it coming. You're correct: despite more flying, more proving, more bargaining, more pleading for relief, the high wore off. Life returned to (my) normal, and Anxiety and Self-doubt and their uncomfortable mates returned to the table. Again.

When I was in primary school, I fell from a set of monkey bars (my mum used to refer to me as a baby elephant because of my lack of grace.) I landed on my back, hard enough to be winded. I lay there staring at the offending structure, with its red paint peeling from all the hands before mine, and gasped for breath between my stinging ribs. I remember this now, because the pain and shock of that fall is exactly how I felt when I realised that the hard feelings weren't going to allow me to get away with One Brave Thing.

One Brave Thing didn't bring me peace.

It turns out that choosing courage once – no matter how big and bold – is no guarantee of an easy ride thereafter. Life asks that we choose brave again. And again.

And so here we are, you and I, working out how we can keep choosing brave when doing so is bloody hard. Seeking out the meaning of it all. Refusing to live on the outskirts. Inviting fear to the table. Letting go of the expectation that courage equals fearlessness. Doing the work anyway. Reminding each other that this is how we expand into a life of our own creation. This is how we dance with inspiration. This is how we break and make ourselves. This is how we bring the peace.

So, let us hold hands with ourselves, and with each other, as we choose brave. Again.

Manifesto for Brave Living

I see you.

The ones living heart wide open. Those driven by the path of their spirit.

Believing love wins. Making room at the table.

Holding hands and space through the process.

You, you trust.

You, you know that you will fall.

And you, you will catch yourself and rise again.

And still, though it hurts, you stay as open as the universe.

I see you.

Graciously allowing fear to be your passenger, while courage drives.

You honour your story: all sacred, all scars.

You are softness and strength. You are persistence and patience. You are healed and still healing.

And you write anew; welcoming beginnings, even if you're not quite ready.

Your intuition is your guru.

When it's hard, you stay. And when it's wrong, you leave.

Sometimes, you make a mess of it.

And still, you forgive yourself as many times as it takes.

You hold it gently.

You've learned humanness is not brokenness.

You know the practice is lifelong. And still, you show up for it.

I see you. I'm with you.

Acceptance

THE BRAVE WAY
IS THROUGH

*A*cceptance is the act of allowing reality to be as it is without resistance, refusal or struggle. It's a place of acknowledgement for the things we can't change, and a channel for reserving our energy for the things we can change. It's a foundation state for courage. We can't do brave things unless we accept discomfort in the first place. That's why I'm starting here in our conversation. Acceptance is the antidote to the struggle with our present reality. It's a summary word for how we move gently through our experience by calling a cease-fire in the war with the painful things we can't control.

But if you're doubting the powers I've just bestowed upon acceptance, I don't blame you. Our default definition doesn't exactly lend itself to being helpful. We assume that acceptance means to give in, give up or give away our personal agency – to lay down in defeat, or worse, to imply we sanction the events that hurt us. That's not the definition I'm referring to in our brave dialogue.

Let me clarify:

Acceptance does not ask you to **approve** of the experience, event, circumstance or feeling.

Acceptance does not ask you to **like** the experience, event, circumstance or feeling.

Acceptance does not ask you to **want** the experience, event, circumstance or feeling.

Let's consider the human condition. It's not that I'm concerned you're questioning your innate reactions – it's more that I'm concerned you might have a habit of being too hard on yourself for things you can't change, control or avoid, given they are a part of your genetic makeup. Your humanness is the reason you have feelings (all of them). And your humanness is also the reason you don't want all the feelings. When emotional discomfort shows up, you react as if you've touched something too hot – you recoil, remove the source of the pain immediately, and reflect on the adverse experience with the intention of not repeating it.

The problem is that uncomfortable feelings linger. We can't just switch the power off.

Even if you're willing to feel some discomfort, you probably do so in a contained way. You do your damnedest to wrap your unpretty feelings in old newspaper and pack them away in boxes in your roof. Maybe you'll unpack those boxes at some stage, late one night while listening to *Jagged Little Pill* (pre-India Alanis). Or maybe you won't, and you'll simply carry the boxes with you to the next house, the next relationship, the next job, the next attempt at habit change.

My point is we automatically reject discomfort, and when we refuse to acknowledge it and work through it, we carry it around in everything that we do.

Discomfort is unwelcome. Your parents told you that. Or maybe it was your third-grade teacher. And your mother-in-law, or the troll who took you down in an Instagram comment, confirmed it: don't feel. And if you do, keep it pretty. Keep it quotable. Keep it private.

But because you're not an android, you're left with the task of steering your way out of the discomfort. You become an emotional hustler, always in a transaction with your pain, jostling for the upper hand. Food, sex, Xanax; gambling, working, *Game of Thrones*; scrolling, smoking, Southern Comfort; achieving, acting, approval-seeking. You trade with agents who anaesthetise the unsettling, uneasy, unlikeable emotions. The problem is they act without prejudice to deaden all feelings. The wounds that caused the feelings are left unaddressed and the messages the feelings are offering go ignored.

But brave doesn't ask you to hide from yourself like that. It asks you to be authentic, which is impossible when you're rejecting any part of yourself. Feelings, memories, mistakes, imperfections – the only way to step into your bravery is through acceptance of your whole self. Even the pieces that you are healing, improving and forgiving. Choosing courage is choosing to accept whatever shows up in the experience of creating the life you want to live.

To cultivate acceptance, try ...

PERSPECTIVE + PATIENCE

PERSPECTIVE

Bring a gentle perspective to the discomfort.
My favourite is the proverb, 'This too shall pass.'
These words are both accepting and hopeful,
allowing the discomfort to be what it is while
acknowledging that all feelings are temporary.

+

PATIENCE

Add to your gentle perspective the conscious step
of choosing patience. When we purposefully choose
patience, it's another pathway out of struggle. Rather
than being at war with the experience, patience allows
us the freedom to simply be with the experience,
however and whenever it shows up.

It's the discomfort of life
that shapes us.

Our scars are the threads
that colour

the tapestry of our
experience.

They make the picture
rich, vibrant.

Acknowledge what hurts.

When you face it
and feel it,

you can then choose
what you do with it.

If you avoid it or
ignore it,

you give your power
to the pain.

You can love well,
work hard and be kind,

but life won't always reward
you accordingly.

Challenges will still arise.

The reward is knowing in
your heart that

you are doing the best you can
with what you've got.

Don't fight the tides of your emotions.

Freedom is found in directing
your energy towards those things
you can control,

and learning to let go of all
that you can't.

Sometimes you need to swim
and sometimes you
just need to float.

Sometimes it's tough.

Not all the time,
just sometimes.

And when you remember
it's only sometimes,

it's a little lighter.

It's going to get hard.

And when it does,
you have the choice

to stay or to walk out
on yourself.

Stay, though.

Give yourself a chance
to see the magic.

No one can dictate how,
what, why or when
you're allowed to feel.

Living fully is an
emotional experience.

You are responsible for how
you respond to your feelings,

but you owe no one an
explanation for feeling
in the first place.

The minute you stop
struggling with your experience,

you can start learning what
it's trying to teach you.

Fighting creates war.

Acceptance invites peace.

Sometimes it's wonderful.

Sometimes it's painful.

Many times, it's in between.

We are all doing our best to navigate our way

through each day as best we can.

Acceptance is trusting
the counterintuitive.

It's trusting stillness in quicksand.

It's trusting forgiveness
in the face of injustice.

It's trusting love in heartbreak.

It's a choice of freedom
over struggle.

Fear

COURAGE TAKES FEAR
BY THE HAND

I'm only half a thumb scroll into my feed and there she is, standing on a mountain top overlooking a majestic view at sunrise. Back to the camera, activewear gleaming, arms outstretched above her head, fingers held in peace signs. The caption is two peaches and a flexed bicep emoji – obviously – but I digress. It's not that she makes me want to go and buy a wardrobe full of shiny new activewear in the hope that my butt will look like hers (it won't) that has me riled. No, butts aside, it's the quote across the bottom of the image in bold sans serif that gets me: 'Once you become fearless, life becomes limitless.'

If this book was a PowerPoint presentation, I'd have a laser pointer all over that statement because I want you to know the truth. You're being deceived about something that affects every single one of us: fear.

We can't talk about courage unless we talk about fear. It's one of the most uncomfortable emotional states we can ever experience. Rightly so, because it's responsible for our survival. Pretty important job. Don't mind fear – it's your brain actively trying to stop you from dying. And this is why I take exception to the number of social media squares that arrive under your thumb advertising the goal of fearlessness.

It's a lie.

The suggestion that we can live without fear is as

seductive as it is destructive. There's no shortage of cultural and media messages that tell us that fearlessness is possible – and required – to reach your full potential. But you're at home feeling anxious about your anxiety. What's wrong with you?

There's nothing wrong with you. We believe in fearlessness because we see others doing brave things and assume they're perfectly confident. We're told they don't feel scared **IN BOLD CAPS** and we assume we're missing a state secret that only the brave and unstoppable have discovered. Know this: unless you have a rare type of brain injury (or you're a psychopath), fearlessness is *impossible*. Fear is your only warning system to navigate the world safely. Trying to turn off your own biology is futile.

And fear is in your corner. It's not intentionally holding you captive, it's simply guarding you from anything it perceives as harmful. Yes, sometimes fear is a little too enthusiastic in its work. Sometimes it locks the gate between you and any new or unfamiliar experience, taking away your opportunity for growth and learning. It promises that if only you stay safe in your comfort zone, it will quieten down. But if you negotiate with fear to be quiet, then you're also giving away your brave. Close your eyes and imagine what kind of life it would be if you were never brave again.

Despite the deceptive title, comfort zones are only comfortable temporarily. Eventually stagnation, boredom and loneliness will find you, supported by a deep intuition telling you that you're robbing yourself of your own life.

In choosing brave, we learn to relate to fear differently. Instead of taking fear's distress signals as fact, we start to question the warnings about failure, shame, rejection or loss. We begin to doubt our doubts. And as we continue to stay the course and do what matters to us deep down, the fear gets quieter (it doesn't leave altogether, but it nags less). Fear realises that not all of its warnings are necessary. This is how we widen our comfort zone. This is what happens when courage shows up.

If you're feeling scared, you know you care. You know it's important. And it's only when you're feeling scared that you need your courage. When you're living in a way that's driven by your values, fear and courage work together. Fear reminds you about things that might hurt you and the things that have hurt you before. Courage reminds you of your strength, your accomplishments, your potential and the possibilities that lie ahead. We need both.

To challenge fear, try ...

LETTING GO OF CONTROL AND TAKING ACTION

If you could control your thoughts and feelings, you wouldn't get stuck. You wouldn't choose to Band-Aid your pain. You'd simply be happy and motivated and calm all the time. (I know, where does this kind of utopia exist?!)

But despite not being able to control your emotional state and mind, you *can* control what you do. Don't believe me? Try this.

I want you to imagine that you can't raise your right arm. Think it as clearly as you can. Now raise your right arm while you're having that thought. You did it, right?

And now think back to a time when you were too tired/ cold/hot/unmotivated to do something, but you did it anyway. Maybe you went for a run on a winter's morning when you didn't feel like it. Maybe you got up and made breakfast for the kids when you didn't feel like it.

We have power over what we do despite the thoughts and feelings that show up in the moment. Even when fear arrives, you can still take brave actions Now, take the fear with you and go and do your brave things!

Remind the parts of
you that are scared,

that the parts of
you that are brave
are here, too.

Even when the fear
of being vulnerable

makes the ground
seem shaky,

the view seem foggy,
and the sky seem dark,

I still want to be a
seeker of personal truth.

I still want to dive deeper.

At that moment,
she was only just
brave enough.
But it was enough.

The walls of your comfort zone
are not only transparent,
they are actually imaginary.

You can cross through them
at any time.

You just have to decide
to take that leap.

When your mind attempts to
run away with your attention,

remember you are neither
time traveller nor fortune teller.

You cannot change yesterday
or predict tomorrow.

The safest anchor is right here
in the present moment.

Sometimes, you'll be
ready to step forward,

to venture outside
your comfort zone,
to face what frightens you.

Other times, you'll choose
to spend a little more
time where you are.

Readiness for growth is
an individual thing.

Go at your own pace.

It's okay to be scared.

Doing something
that's unfamiliar,

like giving yourself
permission to heal,

or follow your dreams,
or be raw and vulnerable,
takes courage.

And courage only
shows up when fear
is present first.

Fear is the
chasm between
where you are now and
where you want to be.

Courage is the bridge
that will help you
cross it.

You're scared
because it matters.

And you're brave
because it matters.

There is a thin line that
sits in between fear and courage
that asks us to balance our
doubts of the unknown with the
pull of discovery.

Fear reminds us of risk.
Courage reminds us of possibility.
We need both.

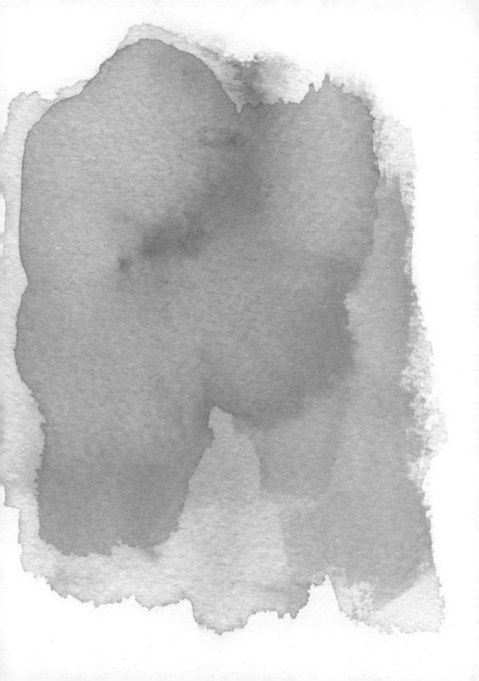

Uncertainty

ALLOW THE UNKNOWN
TO BE SPACIOUS

*T*he brave path would be incredibly congested if it was easy. We'd all stride off down Courageous Road if it was a neat stretch of well-maintained bitumen with helpful signposts along the way, drink stations on every corner and Sherpas to carry our baggage over the hills. You can imagine the number of people keen to claim they'd conquered Courageous Road, requisite Instagram selfie and all, like a travel destination in a list of 100 places to see before you die.

But you already know that your brave path is not on Google maps. You don't get there easily, there's no signage and, if you can find it at all, you'll soon learn that no one is going to deal with your baggage for you (that's kind of the point of doing the work, right?).

The brave path is unknown because you've never been there before. The route is constantly changing as you grow. The landscape is always new, which doesn't sit well with humans who strongly dislike the unknown and unpredict-able (i.e. most of us). The bad news is, if you're going to be anything more than just a tourist on your brave path, then you need to reckon with uncertainty.

While the brave path is where you'll flourish, it's not where you'll go to get comfortable. Courage is a contradic-tion in that way. It's the product of emotional alchemy:

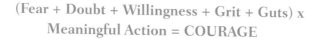

(Fear + Doubt + Willingness + Grit + Guts) x
Meaningful Action = COURAGE

Courage shows up when fear is present first.

Courage is fear plus our doubts about ourselves, the outcome and whether or not we've overstretched.

Courage is fear plus doubt plus the willingness to do something in the face of our uneasiness.

Courage is fear plus doubt plus willingness plus the staying power to see it through when it gets hard.

Courage is fear plus doubt plus willingness plus grit plus the resolve to dare to go beyond.

And most importantly, courage is fear plus doubt plus willingness plus grit plus guts, brought to life by values in action. Courage is not a set of feelings alone. It's a set of feelings that give rise to meaningful action. Brave doesn't just happen by thinking about it (although thinking about it might very well get you to the start line).

You can't choose courage if you won't accept uncertainty as part of the experience. We need it. Without uncertainty, there'd be no reason for mindful footsteps. Instead, we'd stomp surefootedly around without considering the unfamiliar territory ahead. Uncertainty reminds us to act thoughtfully – to be brave, not reckless.

Uncertainty is fear's introverted cousin. It's not in your face, demanding attention like fear. But you'll know it's there, because it has a particular *Have-you-really-thought-this-through?* vibe. It's the space between what we know and what we don't. It's the place where what you need to learn is bigger than what you already know. It feels goosebumpy. A tingly sensation that occurs when you don't know whether to be scared or excited, or curious or resistant, so your skin prickles at the back of your neck in readiness for it all.

In the unknown, you dance with doubt and possibility. It's an opportunity to test out your wings even though there's no guarantee that the landing will be pretty or gentle. You get to choose to stay on the ledge, or to fly anyway, despite the risk.

Not knowing where you'll land doesn't mean you can't take off in the first place. The unknown is spacious, if we're willing to change our relationship with uncertainty to see it as so. Let it invite you into its unfolding. This is where inspiration is born and creativity is fed. This is where brave happens.

To sit with uncertainty, try ...

MAKING ROOM FOR THE FEELINGS

1. Next time you have an unwelcome feeling, observe it as if it had a physical presence inside you.

2. Notice it with non-judgemental curiosity: what shape, colour, size, texture and temperature does it have?

3. Allow the feeling to have space by imagining yourself opening up around it. Each time you inhale, imagine you're expanding around the feeling to give it room.

4. Remember, you don't have to like, want or approve of the feeling. But by allowing the feeling to be present without resistance, you conserve your energy for meaningful and courageous action.

She didn't know when or what or how or why.

She just knew that she trusted herself to learn when the lessons showed up.

The moment that we let go and trust the universe in the face of uncertainty and change, opportunities will show up in the unlikeliest forms and places.

You can't exhale
while you're still holding
your breath.

Freedom sits on the other
side of letting go.

Don't wait so long
to have all the answers
that you miss the
opportunity altogether.

You don't always have
to know why.

Sometimes the point is
what you discover

while you're looking
for the answer,
not the answer itself.

And when it's
all uncertain,

believe in your own
wisdom and your
place on the path.

That's all you need to
know right now.

Sometimes you just need
someone to sit with you
in the silence of not knowing.

To hold your hand and
not grapple for an answer.

And to be present for you
when your mind takes
you elsewhere.

Don't expect to have all
the answers immediately
when you step out of
your comfort zone.

There's always a place
where the learning is
bigger than the knowing.

Allow yourself to move
into the space that is
uncertainty, where you
know you can't go back,

but you're not quite ready
to move forward.

Breathe. Look around.

It may be uncomfortable
but don't rush.

Move forward in your own time.

Maybe there's no easy answer. Maybe there's no answer at all. Maybe your task is to steer into the uncertainty ahead without perfectly understanding what's already been, but choosing to trust the process anyway.

Healing

WE ARE ALL HEALED
AND STILL HEALING

*I*t hurts, I know.

Whatever it is that you're carrying right now, I know the weight of it is tiring and you want nothing more than to put it down, even just for a little while.

'We all have healing work to do.'

Maybe it's the slow, heavy thump of grief. Or the shame that has scarred the edges of your belief in yourself (or someone else). Or the exhausting hustle of anxiety that never switches off. Or the void of lost hope that echoes around your chest. Maybe you don't even have words for it. Some pain is too much for the limitations of language.

Life hurts, and we can't simply put it down when it gets too much. At some point, we will hit the ground from a great height, shatter into a million pieces and then have to find a way to recover the puzzle of ourselves.

Along with loving and hurting, healing is a common thread that binds us to each other. We are all healed, and still healing – this is what helps us connect. It helps us be more empathic. It helps us accept that we are all the same. We are all broken and put back together more beautiful than before (albeit with a few parts that might remain a little fragile).

We all have healing work to do. And none of us likes it. And pain is unpredictable, which makes healing an imprecise venture. Some wounds take a lifetime of perpetual tending and are prone to flare up occasionally. Others heal but leave a scar. And some close over so that we may never even recall that they were bruised in the first place.

I can't tell you what yours will look like. But I can tell you that it probably won't look like you expect it to. The intensity and timeframe of suffering doesn't usually conform to our rules, or those of the people around us. It can't always be patched up with a tidy little blister-pack of medication. So, no – there's no perfect prescription for healing for you specifically. Part of the task of putting ourselves back together is to discover what works at the time we need it to.

Where are you at with your healing? You might not find the right thing in the right place with the right person on the first try. But you will find it at some point, and the healing will be a salve and a saviour at once. It's unlikely to be smooth, though. It's never a linear process. So allow yourself to get off track. Placing expectations and demands on your healing will have you forcing things that shouldn't be forced and giving up when you need to keep going. Disentangling pain requires room and flexibility and permission and, most of all, a willingness to find your way through the knots – however that happens.

I'm not saying you need to go to extraordinary lengths to

find your healing, either. You don't have to go and meditate in a cave for three years or pay a fortune to stay at a health spa in a far-off land (although that kind of Eden would be nice to visit every now and then!). I'm simply saying when you make room for the healing you need right now, the transformation begins to take shape. What hurts begins to hurt a little less because you're there, doing the work.

Healing is the work of the brave. It demands we face up to the bits that are breaking down and the bits that have been long broken. It demands we commit to moving through the pain rather than around it. It demands that we commit to ourselves, even when the light at the end of the tunnel is from a torch we hold for ourselves.

Healing is the way we make it beautiful again.

To nurture your healing, try ...

SPEAKING THE PAIN ALOUD

Our wounds have greater power over us in the dark. This is as true for the long nights of anxiety or loneliness or grief (hello, 3 am mind flip out) as it is for pain that remains unspoken. Pain loses some of its power when it's talked about, brought into the light and shared in a safe way. Speak of your pain and to your pain in the company of someone you trust. But please choose your person wisely. There's nothing more damaging to a healing process than someone invalidating your experience.

Shine a light on what hurts, and you'll find that its strength dissipates when completely acknowledged, no longer able to gnaw at you in secret.

Give it a label. If it's sadness, call it Sadness. This way it becomes simply a part of your experience in this moment, rather than an unidentified shadow over your entire being. Be brave and speak your truth.

THINGS I KNOW ABOUT HEALING:

It gets harder before
it gets easier.

We must participate.

It's worth it.

I don't know how
long healing takes.

I only know that
it starts with
acknowledging that
you are worthy
exactly as you are.

She showed up.

She brought all the
willingness.

And she was the healing
she needed.

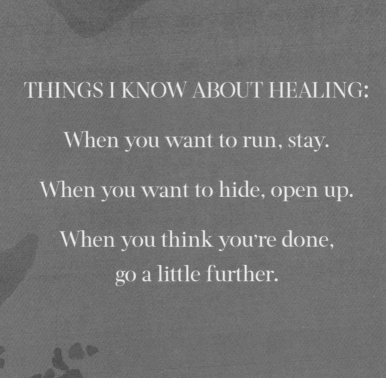

THINGS I KNOW ABOUT HEALING:

When you want to run, stay.

When you want to hide, open up.

When you think you're done,
go a little further.

Don't judge the healing process.

It will bring you what you need
when you need it, even if you
don't realise you need it.

But only if you're willing.

THINGS I KNOW ABOUT HEALING:

You get to set the pace,
no one else.

You get to define what growth
looks like for you.

You get to start over as
many times as it takes.

You can be
healed and still healing.

You can be
open and still hurting.

You can be
brave and still frightened.

THINGS I KNOW ABOUT HEALING:

Speaking kindly
to yourself helps.

A lot.

She didn't know that her
heart could break like that.

But until it did,
she didn't know that she
knew how to put
the pieces back together,

and see it as more
beautiful than before.

THINGS I KNOW ABOUT HEALING:

Forgiving yourself helps.

A lot.

Courage

THE UNIVERSE LISTENS
TO BRAVE

*M*y pop passed away a few months ago. He was 89 and desperate to be free of the pain that ravaged him, while simultaneously devastated and shocked that his life was being 'cut short'. He would've loved another 89 years, such was his zest for life.

My nan held her husband of 69 years in the moment that he passed. I'm convinced a piece of her soul left with him that day, refusing to stay in a world where he was no longer. I could see it in her eyes: the wretchedness of parting was worse than any earthly or physical pain she'd experienced in her 90 years.

But did she tell me she wished she'd never loved Pop because the grief was simply unbearable? No. Instead, Nan wiped my tears and said, 'Darling, in the end, all that matters is who we love, and how we love them.'

This is brave living. To choose the suffering all over again because the profound beauty is worth it.

You'll find your courage at the altar where discomfort marries caring. Where what matters overcomes what hurts. It's here that the risk of failure, rejection, judgement and shame becomes acceptable in the service of living by what truly matters.

Brave is about feeling uncomfortable for a purpose. It's about making the discomfort worth something. But it's up to you to determine what that something will be. I can't define your values for you, but I can tell you that you'll find them on the other side of your suffering. And if you say that your suffering is blinding, I'd say bring your curiosity to it. Allow yourself to wonder what all the fuss is about, because I bet that your heart is trying to tell you something is up. It's trying to tell you what you care about.

> Brave is to live rather than hide.
> Brave is to explore rather than stay put.
> Brave is to be authentic rather than pre-approved.
> Brave is effortful and enduring and earnest.

But please don't buy into the idea that courage only rates if it's extra-large on some invisible scale of brave acts. It's the fact that you opened the door of your comfort zone and stepped outside – not how far you went – that matters. One person's Everest is another person's 'I love you'. My brave cannot be compared to your brave. We're too unique for that.

Before you tell me that you'll be brave when you finally feel ready to do The Thing, please know this: courage doesn't turn up just because you've waited around long enough. (Okay, it might, but who has that kind of time?)

The thing is you might have to take action before you are perfectly ready to do so.

But perhaps you haven't realised how brave you already are? Do you realise that brave is tiny acts in the service of surviving, as well as giant acts in the service of strength and resilience? That every brave action counts even when no one is there to witness it?

I'm inviting you to see the courage already within you. And I'm inviting you to do your thing *before* you're ready, because choosing safety and staying comfortable is a compromise of your very essence. What would life look like if you bought into fear's stories? What would you miss out on? Is safety worth it if it means participating in the destruction of your spirit?

Listen to the brave whispers.

What will you stand for?

What will be said about how you lived when those closest to you gather to celebrate your life?

What will you create with your remaining years to say you lived bravely?

Say you'll love your people and do your things and stand up for what you believe in. That's what courage wants to hear.

BRAVE RITUAL

To find your courage, try ...

MAKING IT A DAILY PRACTICE

Please don't wait around until you feel brave to start taking brave actions. Feelings are not predictable, and if your courageous acts are dependent on all your feelings aligning to get you over the proverbial start line, you may be waiting a long time.

Practise courage the same way you might practise playing piano – a little bit each day. The more you practise stepping forward despite your fears, the more your brain learns that many fears are unnecessary and the bigger your brave grows.

Note down your daily brave actions in your diary, notebook or on your phone. The act of recording the action or feeling will help cement the ritual. Sometimes it will be as simple as 'I showed up today'.

Daily practice makes courage a habit. Start small and build upon those things. The more expansive your life becomes, the deeper and richer your experience will be.

She was never
quite ready.

But she was brave.

And the Universe
listens to brave.

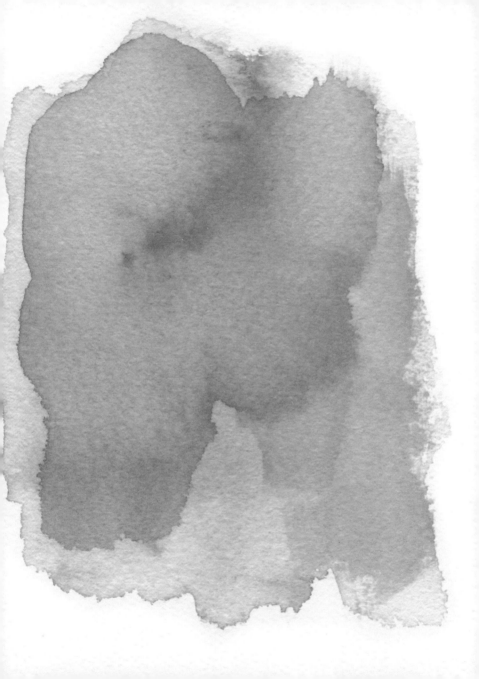

Courage is not being 'fearless'.

Courage is shaking at the knees,
choking on your words,
heart gripped by uncertainty,

but stepping forward on your
journey anyway.

Courage takes fear
by the hand
and shows it how
to turn into growth.

Please acknowledge every quiet,
small, unseen act of courage
that brought you to now.

The gradual reopening of your heart
after it fractured.

The awakening into a necessary,
difficult healing.

The turning away from self-doubt.

This is bravery.

Finally, she was
tired of running.

So, she used her
brave instead.

Please don't think you must
be fearless on your path.

Fear walks ahead, anticipating
where the terrain is rough
and navigating what's unfamiliar.

Courage is the light that
catches us from behind,
and pushes us forward
beyond where fear can see.

We need both.

Courage is not closing down
and denying yourself hope.

Courage is being tender with
your vulnerability

and acknowledging how much
you want it, whatever it is.

Courage is also believing in
your own strength
no matter how it turns out.

Brave is when
you're actually doing it.

(Not just thinking about it.)

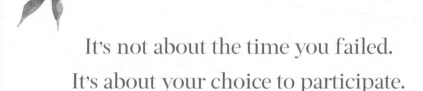

It's not about the time you failed.
It's about your choice to participate.

It's not about the time your heart broke.
It's about your choice to love.

It's not about the time you were scared.
It's about you choosing brave.

Go with your dreams.

Even when others don't.
Or won't.

Even when you quake
and shake.

Even when you doubt
what's possible.

Because living bravely
is doing it anyway.

And to ignore your brave
is to ignore your truth.

Hope

HOPE, SHE HAS A
DETERMINED VOICE

*R*emaining hopeful is a revolutionary act in a world that gives us too many reasons not to hope. It might be rebellious to put your belief in something better, but it's not foolish. It's exactly that belief that brings about change at a personal, community and global level.

I get it – the darker things become, the more fragile our sense of hope can be. It's much easier to sit in despair and resignation where the walls are solid and feel permanent. Reaching out to hope feels flimsy and requires faith in the intangible.

But hope is a flotation device. Give it a chance and it's the thing that will take your weight when you're convinced you're sinking. It will save you from the storm and from yourself – if you allow its presence. The voice of hope speaks to the impermanence of everything: feelings, transitions, hardships, blessings. Hope allows us to let it all come and let it all go, and let it come again if, and when, it's meant to.

Don't get me wrong, I'm not saying you have to believe in hope 100 per cent of the time. In fact, your relationship with hope may be tenuous at the very time you need her most. It's easy to be angry with her and to choose the far more practical and protective attitudes of pessimism and scepticism. After all, you've been hurt before. What's to say that this time will be any different?

Maybe you've judged hope as fickle, discriminatory and unjust because of the painful experiences you've suffered. But hope is determined. She will continue to call to you. When we forget to listen it's because we lose sight of our options. Hope *is* an option, though. She may not be your default option, but she's the option that will carry you forward. Looking forward asks that you allow something else to be present that you don't yet have clarity around or access to. That 'something else' is the possibility for something better.

Hope brings the light, even to light-filled things. You are allowed to hope when things are going well, do you know that? You are allowed to hope for your deepest wishes – the ones that you only tell a select few so that these dreams remain untainted by negativity. For anything that gives you a sense of purpose and meaning, hope has a rightful and necessary place as part of its creation.

Because without hope, how do we try?

Without hope, how do we fall and get back up, and try again?

We need to give ourselves permission to hope for the things most precious to us – even in the face of our own resistance, resistance from others, and resistance from a society that tells us what we should hope for. Even while darkness exists in the world, we must bring hope to what's good.

Sometimes the hope you need is within you, but not always. Sometimes, it shows up as timely encouragement from a friend, or the page in a book that spoke to you at just the right time. Maybe it's a piece of art that showed you another perspective. And maybe, it's in someone that reminded you of the parts of yourself that you had forgotten to acknowledge: the parts that are strong, brave, soft and willing.

Be open to whatever form hope may choose to live through on her visit to you.

Look harder for her.

Listen closely to her.

I promise you she is there, ready to show you the light and take the weight and remind you to breathe.

To find hope, try...

LOOKING, LISTENING AND FEELING FOR HOPE AROUND YOU

Fill up moments that feel devoid of hope with the beauty of life around you. Because hopelessness is such an all-encompassing state, it can obscure our view of anything joyful or beautiful.

Look for hope on purpose.
Listen for hope on purpose.
Feel for hope on purpose.

Go for a walk and note the natural beauty of your surroundings. Take in the sky, the trees, the birds and the ground under your feet.

If you are on the train or bus, put down your phone and instead observe those around you. If you look hard enough, you will see small kindnesses everywhere.

Perhaps you'll see her in the turn of the season from winter to spring. Perhaps you'll hear her in a kind word spoken to you, or exchanged between strangers. Perhaps you'll feel her in a moment of gratitude. She's there, but sometimes you have to find her on purpose.

Perhaps it's meant to
be unfinished right now.

Not everything gets
perfectly completed.

If it's meant to have
a different ending,

you'll find your way
back to it.

You can always tell the
feelings that work the hardest
by the mess they show up in.

Hope – she is the one
ready with boots on.

She's got dirt under her nails
and sweat on the back of her neck.

She will be there with you
sifting through the wreckage.

And Hope – she's the one
who helps you pick up the pieces
and rebuild it all.

Stuck is not a destination.

It's a point in time.

A tide in the process.

A passing through,
always on the way
to unstuck.

When gazing in the
direction of your past,

don't forget to marvel
at all the times
you've walked with
courage, strength,
determination and heart.

How else do you think
you made it this far?

It's okay to grieve for an
end and welcome a
beginning all at once.

You can miss what's
been and look forward
to what's to come
in the same moment.

I don't know what the future
is going to look like.

But I do know that the one you
participate in creating

will look very different
from the one that
you let happen to you.

Don't be surprised at
how quickly the universe
will move with you
once you have decided.

We don't always come
to healing willingly.

Instead, we fight and claw
to stay inside the prison of our own
pain, convincing ourselves
we can't help it.

Familiarity is persuasive
like that.

But Hope has a determined voice.
She will keep calling you.

If you haven't found it yet,

that may not mean what you're
making it mean.

Perhaps its time has not yet arrived.

Perhaps it's already here but
looks different than you expected.

Perhaps you need to
let go or turn a corner first.

Or perhaps you need a break
from searching
to see clearly again.

Hope is not a fool.
She doesn't promise it won't hurt.

Or that it will be easy.
She doesn't even tell you the way.

But she does remind you that
it matters.

And as long as you are seeking,
Hope is listening.

Rise

YOU CAN FALL, BUT YOU CAN
CATCH YOURSELF, TOO

*T*here's nothing more beautiful than a woman who has honoured herself by doing the work. Beauty is a woman who has bowed to her pain, taken the lessons it has offered and transformed it into a version of herself that she loves. That's power. That's rising.

But it's not easy. It's not pleasant. And the things that cause us to fall are never things we'd voluntarily sign up for in the first place. No one wishes for the heartache of rejection, loss, shame or judgement. No one wishes for their brave things to fail.

But sometimes they do.

Sometimes we do.

If you find yourself on the ground right now, I want to remind you that you can't possibly rise unless you're on the ground in the first place. Falling does not mean failing. It means you have tried for something. It's the surest sign you chose the side of brave. Your resurgence, your growth and your tomorrow are defined by how you recover and get back up again.

Although it may not feel like it at the point of impact, the ground is a blessing. (Don't worry, I'm not about to launch into a 'just think positive' platitude.) The ground breaks the fall at the point where you need a course correction. You may not realise it at the time – the frustrating thing

'You are not in competition with anyone else, or even previous versions of yourself.'

for those of us that struggle with impatience (my hand is raised) is that hindsight doesn't develop overnight. But the process of getting back up starts with the ground earthing you. Holding you. Giving you the stability on which to rest while you repair what needs to be repaired within yourself. It makes no demands that you get back up immediately. It simply offers you a foundation for renewal.

I'm convinced the success of our rising comes from our willingness to use mindful and gentle hands as we reassemble ourselves. To put ourselves back together kindly, compassionately and encouragingly, and to surrender to the experience as a necessary juncture on the way to emerging triumphant from the ashes.

There is no rush. You don't have to move mountains. You can make a series of small, brave movements towards trying again in your own time. You are not in competition with anyone else, or even previous versions of yourself. This is new growth – cultivate it tenderly.

Making sense of painful experiences is sacred. Go gently.

But it doesn't have to be all encompassing. Know that you can thrive in one area of life while you're simultaneously reassembling pieces of yourself in another. Emotions are not mutually exclusive. We can't simply put life on hold

while we work through one feeling at a time.

But what if the ground seems shaky? What if your faith in yourself is hard to grasp right now? This is the point where I want you to remember the fire inside you. I want you to remember every time you didn't think you'd survive the pain, and yet here you are. Every time you found the strength, determination and wisdom to relight your spirit so that you're here reading this today. I want you to remember you *will* get back up – because you always have.

We rise and then we believe in ourselves. We believe in ourselves and then we rise again.

Show me anyone who has been through hell and not been burned.

Show me anyone who picked themselves up from the ground and didn't look back in awe at what they were able to rebuild, despite the obstacles.

Show me anyone who has risen.

And I'll show you brave.

🌿 BRAVE RITUAL 🌿

To rise, try ...

COMPASSIONATE LANDINGS +
COURAGEOUS BEGINNINGS

It's far easier to get back up after a fall when the landing is soft. Bring compassion to yourself in times of failure and disappointment. Remind yourself of your strengths. Remind yourself of the importance of trying. Hold space for yourself while you recover. Speak to yourself kindly and respectfully. This is the place for encouragement and learning, not criticism and shaming. Self-compassion in times of defeat provides you with the most stable, warm and reassuring platform to start again. The way you catch yourself in the fall determines how and when you'll fly again.

Start by saying these offerings to yourself:

1. My mistakes don't define me.
2. I am loved.
3. I make a difference by _____.
4. I am allowed to forgive myself.
5. It's time to let go of _____ because I've carried it for long enough.
6. I honour the parts of myself that still hurt.
7. I am strong and capable.
8. I showed up today, and that's what counts.
9. I acknowledge myself for doing hard things.
10. I will keep going. I've got this.

ADD YOUR OWN:

1. _____

2. _____

It's about believing
in yourself.

That even when you
don't know how,
you'll figure it out.

She's learned to remind
herself that she'll be okay.

Because she's proved
that she always is.

She's got that kind of spirit
that just can't be extinguished.

You will fall.

But every time you
gather your pieces
together and rise again,

you'll learn that you are
always going to be okay.

You can fall down,
but you can catch
yourself, too.

She learned to stop
walking out on herself.
To stop letting herself down.

So, she stayed when it got hard.

She believed in
her own capacity to rise.

She saw it happen.

And vowed to never stop
believing in herself again.

And the moment came
when she had to undecide
things about herself that she'd
previously considered true.

It was time to honour growth.

It was time to see the change.

She was no longer that Self.

She had created herself anew.

If you didn't have an
infinite capacity to rise,
you wouldn't have
made it this far along
your path.

If nothing else,
believe in that.

Believe in your inner
phoenix.

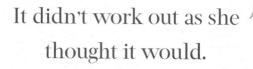

It didn't work out as she
thought it would.

And it hurt like hell.

But she's got that kind
of quiet strength.

The one that resolves to start
again tomorrow.

The one that acknowledges
herself for trying.

The one that will get her
everywhere she needs to go.

You should see her
since she gave herself
permission to rise.

Her rise was so stunning,
you could tell she'd
been broken more
than once.

You know that time
you fell and you caught
yourself?

That was beautiful.

Do that again.

Trust

YOUR INNER SENSE

*I*want to shine a light on your inner world, and in particular, the sense only present within you as intangible vibrations and voice. Whether we call it intuition, gut feeling, sixth sense or instinct, this is the sense that represents trust – trust in yourself, in what's happening around you and in the process at large.

Everyone has intuition, but not everyone seeks it out. Not everyone cultivates it, respects it or considers it an essential part of the journey. Some people have a close relationship with their intuition, checking in regularly for guidance to confirm what feels right. Others are disconnected from their intuition, either because they don't value it as a source of information, or because they've experienced what it's like to let themselves down.

If you're tight with your intuition, you'll already know about the gift of your own wisdom and guidance. Trust is earned through actions. The way we build trust in ourselves is the same way that we come to trust others: through small actions that demonstrate we'll show up when we're needed. But what if you're not sure you can trust yourself because it's gone wrong previously? What if you've ignored your better judgement and done something you regret? There's nothing like walking out on yourself to trigger that unsettling feeling that you can no longer hear, let alone trust, your instincts. Reconnecting with our intuition is how we become more than the pieces that fell apart in the first place. And it's here that we stop looking outside for approval, assuming others know what's best for us. It's precisely because of the mistakes we've made that we know what we know now.

You see, you can't know what you don't know yet. You're negotiating your way through the world as best you can with the knowledge and awareness you have today. That means you can't apply insights you came to this month to the choices you made last month, let alone in 2005.

One of the ways we level up in life is by learning what doesn't work. This kind of wisdom is only available via our missteps. Keeping yourself enslaved by your mistakes, infinitely condemned, is not attaining wisdom. It's self-flagellation that stonewalls your growth and paralyses you from making right what's gone wrong, and then moving forward.

Intuition strengthens the more we listen to it, the more we ask it to contribute. Please don't disregard one of the most powerful forms of guidance you have, all because you stopped for a minute to learn something about yourself that you didn't know previously.

Collaborating with your intuition allows you to open up

to something bigger than yourself. To leave some of the process up to universal energy, letting go of the pressure to understand everything right now and, instead, trusting that it's unfolding as it's meant to. You retain your agency over what you can directly control, while simultaneously bringing patience to your own evolution.

Take this where it fits. I know I move more softly through the world when I release my urge to control everything.

But I have only learned this by losing trust. I found trust in myself by walking out when I needed me most, and then coming back in the nick of time. I found trust in something bigger by realising that carrying only that which is tangible failed to account for too much and left me nearly collapsing under the weight of having to take charge and manage it all.

You're allowed to ask for help from yourself. Your intuition knows the way. War cannot continue to exist if you keep bringing the peace. And we bring the peace through trust.

BRAVE RITUAL

To build trust, try ...

RECONNECTING WITH
YOUR INNER SENSE

1. Find a place where you can sit quietly for a few minutes without interruption.

2. If it's a place where you feel inspired and peaceful, even better.

3. Sit in stillness. Reduce the information you have to process visually and mentally by closing your eyes and turning off any devices.

4. Follow your breath. Minds like to chat and solve problems. They don't like to be quiet, so give your mind something to do by observing or counting your breath.

5. Sit in stillness and listen closely for your inner voice.

It might take regular practice, but this exercise will bring you back to yourself and allow you to hear what your inner sense is trying to communicate to you.

There came a time when
she no longer chased approval.

Her intuition proved a far
wiser guide than the whim of
another's opinion.

She chose to trust herself.

She learned to distinguish
the quiet whisper of her intuition
from the incessant chatter of
her mind.

The more she listened,
the more she heard.

MIND

'I want to get to know you.'

HEART

'You already do.'

SOUL

'If only you'd listen.'

There's only so long you can
ignore the whisper of your intuition
before it becomes inaudible.

It's always there, but you'll never
hear it as long as you choose to listen
to everyone else before
you listen to yourself.

HEART

'Follow me.'

MIND

'Can I see the map?'

SOUL

'I trust you.'

Just because it hasn't happened yet
doesn't mean you're not cut out for it.

Or that it's not meant for you.
Listen to your intuition.

And remember that
impatience is rarely
a good adviser.

THINGS YOU DON'T NEED
PERMISSION FOR:

1. Trusting your wisdom.

2. Trusting your truth.

3. Trusting your capacity to
   choose for yourself.

Let it go … even when you're not sure what's next.

Sometimes we need to create an empty space before we can decide what will fill it.

The universe moves when you do.

(But you have to move first.)

I know you're doing everything
you can to get there.

Shepherding your energy towards
what you can control.

Applying a little faith.

Accepting what you can't change.

Softening into the journey.

Letting go of the outcome.

This is the flow. Here you are,
flowing with it.

Kin

CONNECTION TO A
BRAVE COLLECTIVE

*C*onnection is in our DNA. Our brains are wired to keep us close to one another, and to reward us with large doses of oxytocin (the love hormone) when we are side by side. There's a reason this need for belonging has so much power over us: connection is a fundamental contributor to positive mental health. Without social interaction, a sense of being part of a group and some sense of feeling loved, we become life-alteringly unwell. It's a non-negotiable need.

We do whatever we need to do to belong, thanks to the strength of our biology (even when trying to belong compromises our authenticity, our first instinct is to do what needs to be done to fit in). Our preoccupation with judgement and approval from others stems from our time roaming the earth in clans. We people-please, try to keep up with the Joneses and constantly compare ourselves, because once upon a time fitting in meant that our people would protect us (or would reject us if we failed to do so). Approval equalled survival. Those times have long passed, but our ancestral drives are hard to unlearn.

What I'm saying is we need each other, as we always have, but for much more than just survival now. When we're out trying to live the brave life, we need the ones who encourage us to do so, while also pursuing their own courageous things. This is your brave collective.

Here's why.

When you are living bravely, not everyone will support or understand your intentions, actions and efforts. Working on your growth can be a threat to those who are choosing safety. For those around you who resist change and evolution, holding you back or tearing you down protects them from having to look in a mirror at their own stagnation. There is no way you can embody your own bravery completely if you're too busy managing the people around you who are determined to snuff out the fire you're actively working to keep alight. (While we're here, it's worth checking in with yourself with the question: 'Who am I holding back? Who am I trying to keep safe so that I also feel safe?'.)

In your brave collective, you'll be surrounded by those who don't problem-solve to fix your fear, but instead help you explore whether you're feeling fear in the service of doing something important. When it gets hard, they'll remind you that nothing important gets done without a decent level of gut-churning and knee-shaking. They'll remind you that creating and loving and living authentically is overwhelmingly preferable to hiding away and giving in to shame and doubt.

And by collective, I don't mean you need 100 friends to hang out with on a Friday night (the introvert in me shudders in horror!). But I do mean that you need a couple of people

whose opinions you trust. Who will sit beside you while you do the work of creating and failing and learning and growing; who will tell you the truth gently and constructively; and who refuse to allow you to be anything less than your most beautiful potential.

Courage is contagious, but so are fear and apathy. Who you spend time with matters. Stay with those who continuously choose safety and familiarity, or those who couldn't care less about doing something meaningful with their lives, and you risk being influenced by those attitudes. Do you really want to put that kind of obstacle in front of you when there are already enough walls to climb in between here and brave action?

When you find your brave collective, you'll be inspired to go further than ever before because shared courage is more powerful than courage that lives only in the quiet of our minds. You'll be supported to strive, to challenge the status quo. And more importantly, when it doesn't work out, you'll find a gentle space to fall and recover among people who have been there.

For brave living, there is nothing more essential than those who stand behind you, reminding you it's worth it. Choose the ones who choose courage for themselves, and for you, too. Go and find them. You'll know them by the welcome they give you. That's where you belong.

To find your brave collective, try ...

REACHING OUT

Seek out your people for their support, encouragement, reassurance and butt-kicking skills when you need them.

Ask them to keep you on track.

Ask them to remind you of your reasons for being courageous when you forget.

Ask them to back you, but not to let you cop out and trip yourself up.

And if you aren't sure who your people are, find the ones who are out there being brave in the ways you want to be brave. Find where they're doing their brave things and join them. That's where you'll connect with the ones who will see you for you and love you for it.

Not everyone will be supportive of your journey to better yourself.

Some people are threatened by change because it holds up a mirror they would rather not see.

Only you need to understand your reasons for moving forward.

Here's to all the people who
have dressed their own wounds,

tended to their own bruises
and stayed open.

Here's to the ones who refuse
to close down

but instead choose possibility,
love and new beginnings.

I seek out the ones
who are in the middle of it.

The middle of making.

The middle of healing.

The middle of learning.

The middle of changing.

Because I know how much courage it takes
to get from a beginning to a middle,
and then stay there to do the work.

Don't let the
judgements, expectations
or opinions of others
make you give away
your courage.

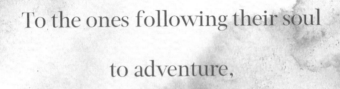

To the ones following their soul

to adventure,

to heal,

to seek,

to expand:

I see you. I'm with you.

The ones who know
that following your
dreams means fear in
your throat and courage
in your belly?

Those ones are
my people.

I see you there.

Showing up and trying
and pushing through.

Choosing forward over stuck.

Holding your own hand
when it gets hard.

Learning to love yourself first.
You're my kind of people.

The ones who know you're brave
even in the quiet, unseen times;
the ones who remind you
to exhale,

and who remind you
that feelings are always just
passing through?

They're the ones to hold onto.

Your brave
inspires my brave.

It's a special kind
of person
of person

who forgives
your fall

and cheers for
your revival.

Journey

GO GENTLY. NOW, GO.

*I*f you are still anticipating your first step towards your next big brave thing, now is the time to take it. Go now. Go gently, but please go. There is no reason to keep waiting. I'll just leave these reminders here as you get on your way:

1. Your journey will look as it is meant to look for you. There is no right way for it to pan out. Don't judge it, but don't hide from it either.

2. Commit to the journey. Commit to feeling what you have to feel to move through it. Commit to doing what you have to do to transform. Commit to those around you and their growth.

3. Judgement, criticism, expectation and comparison are toxic. Go your own way (you're going the right way).

4. Allow yourself to be stuck. Allow yourself to run. Allow yourself to resist. These are all essential waypoints on the purposeful path.

5. Start, even if you're not quite ready.

6. Sometimes it's hard. But not all the time. In the spaces between, never forget there is unbridled joy, excitement, satisfaction, contentment, the deepest love and the greatest awe waiting for you on the brave journey. Don't ignore these elements. Don't miss the colour.

7. The start is always difficult. The middle is always messy. The ending is always a new version of beauty.

8. You can't predict what it will look like, how long it will take, who will show up, who will leave, or what you'll discover along the way. But every part is necessary.

9. You will get better at staying with courage and doing courageous things.

10. You're not late. You're never too late.

11. Don't make it harder than it needs to be. Overthinking is not useful. And yes, you are enough.

12. You're not supposed to like it all the time.

13. You'll need help for some parts.

14. Many people won't understand. Many people won't even notice. The ones who do understand and notice are your brave collective.

15. Courage feels familiar and unfamiliar at the same time – this is because being brave reintroduces us to our true selves.

16. You'll cop out and try and convince yourself that you're being brave (but deep down you'll know that's bullshit and that you have to get out of your own way).

17. The pain is real. So is the healing. And the transformation.

18. No one can do it for you.

19. No one can tell you how to do it (and everyone has an opinion).

20. You have to practise (everything).

21. There's more to come that you can't know and the stuff that you already know matters.

22. You won't necessarily understand it the first time. Some things you won't understand until years later.

23. You have to stay with yourself, back yourself and trust yourself. But that won't be easy.

24. Everything is easier said than done. Everything.

25. What's going on within you matters more than what's going on around you.

26. Brave means taking action.

Now go, lovely one. Go and do your brave things. Go gently. But please, GO!

BRAVE RITUAL

To start your journey, try ...

DEFINING YOUR PATH

Grab a pen and some paper and take yourself to
a spot that makes your heart feel light and your mind
feel expansive. Write down what it would look like if
you were living your bravest life.

You may not have all the answers, but write down
the parts that you can see in your mind right now.
What are you doing more of? What are you doing
less of? How are you loving the people close to you?
What do you say yes to, and when do you say no?
What's possible when you're being brave?

Once you've written down your thoughts, read back over
them and look for the first small steps you can take in the
service of being courageous. Remember that uncertainty
and fear will be present. You may not have any guarantees
or even any idea of how things will turn out. But you can
still take brave action. You can still start now!

Transition into this new
chapter gently.

There's no need to rush or force it.

Give yourself time to try it on.
See what fits.

And leave a little room
for movement.

Amazing things need room
to grow.

Create. Grieve. Change. Heal.

Whatever it is, move into it.

It won't look like you expect it to.

It will be harder, longer and
messier than you think.

But the process will be life-altering,

and the result will be
unimaginably beautiful.

You don't need
permission to
walk away from what's
not working.

But you do need
self-respect.

If it's not working, work harder.

If you have worked on it as hard
as you can, then walk away.

It may not be a matter
of life or death,
but staying stuck will certainly
starve your soul and injure
your heart.

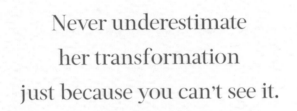

Never underestimate
her transformation
just because you can't see it.

The cover may look the same
while her story is being
completely rewritten.

You can be stuck and
still in progress.

You can be authentic
and still transforming.

You can be decided
and still wondering.

And even though the
healing hurt,

she couldn't help but
marvel at the beauty

of her own
transformation.

Some things unfold gently.

Forgiveness.

Trust.

Healing.

Self-belief.

Don't rush these things,
they are seeds for your growth.

It can hurt

to shed one layer of yourself

to get to the next.

We simply cannot grow

without the discomfort of change.

But the beauty is not just in the result,

but in the shaping of the result:

you and the magic of transformation.

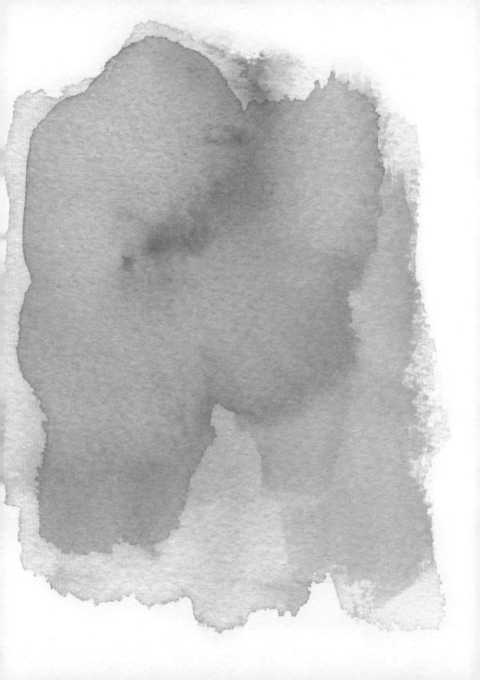

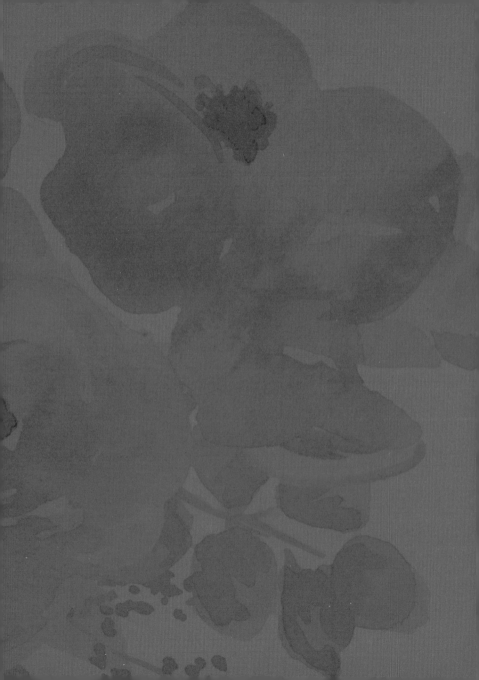

I'd rather graze my knees
in the gravel of my mistakes,
than hide from life and stay untouched.
I want my breath to shake and
my gut to churn.

I want to call to the stars that I am living,
showing my heart what is really possible.

Again,

we are

brave

And again, we're brave.

Again, we step forward, even when we're not ready.

Again, we stay to do the work.

Again, we evolve into more inspired and expansive versions of ourselves.

Keep going.

I see you. I'm with you.

Choose brave.

The universe is listening.

A FEW WORDS OF GRATITUDE

*M*y endless thanks belong first and foremost to my people: the ones who have received my words with willing hearts, open minds and souls thirsty for brave connection. On screens and on pages, you have given me the gift of company on this path as we keep seeking and finding together. I see you. I'm with you. It's your brave that inspires my brave.

For showing me what real love is and for being my biggest source of inspiration and courage. For always having my back and for staying through the rough parts. For introducing me to myself gently when I'm an elephant in a china shop and for disentangling the knots I get myself into sometimes. For being the kindest, bravest, strongest woman I know – and gently sending me back to my keyboard when I threaten to give up. There are no thanks significant enough for my wife, Nyssa. Instead, you get every chamber of my heart and the map to our family's future, always.

Thank you to Bennett for reminding me that picking up a strawberry by yourself for the first time and delivering it to your mouth is where it's at. That perfect beauty is always found in the most precious and simple things. Thank you for choosing us and keeping me brave.

To my mum and dad – I know you don't always understand my methods or goals, or the fact that I lead with my heart first and head second, but I am so grateful that you back me anyway, giving me the freedom and respect to walk my own path. (And Mum: sending countless copies of my books to your friends is the greatest compliment I could ever receive.) I know how lucky I am to have you both.

Thank you to my agent, Clare, who continues to believe in my work and purpose, and to my publishing team at Pan Macmillan: especially Ingrid, for your enthusiasm from the outset; Virginia, for the incredible attention, respect and ever-so-gentle assembly of my words; and Alissa, for your breathtaking design. Thank you for such a beautiful experience in bringing this book together.

I am brave because of each of you. Thank you.

First published 2019 in Macmillan
by Pan Macmillan Australia Pty Limited
1 Market Street, Sydney, New South Wales
Australia 2000

A CIP catalogue record for this book is available from the National
Library of Australia: http://catalogue.nla.gov.au

Design by Alissa Dinallo
Colour + reproduction by Splitting Image Colour Studio
Printed in China by Imago

We advise that the information contained in this book does not negate personal
responsibility on the part of the reader for their own health and safety. It is
recommended that individually tailored advice is sought from your healthcare or
medical professional. The publishers and their respective employees, agents and
authors are not liable for injuries or damage occasioned to any person as a result
of reading or following the information contained in this book.

10 9 8 7 6 5 4 3 2 1